Developing Numeracy
SOLVING PROBLEMS
ACTIVITIES FOR THE DAILY MATHS LESSON

year R

Christine Moorcroft

A & C BLACK

Contents

Problems involving 'real life'

Problems involving money

Reprinted 2001, 2002, 2004, 2005, 2006, 2007
First published 2000 by A & C Black Publishers Limited
38 Soho Square, London WID 3HB
www.acblack.com

ISBN 978-0-7136-5443-1

Copyright text © Christine Moorcroft, 2000
Copyright illustrations © Michael Evans, 2000
Copyright cover illustration © Charlotte Hard, 2000
Editors: Lynne Williamson and Marie Lister

The authors and publishers would like to thank the following teachers for their advice in producing this series of books: Stuart Anslow; Jane Beynon; Cathy Davey; Ann Flint; Shirley Gooch; Barbara Locke; Madeleine Madden; Helen Mason; Fern Oliver; Jo Turpin.

A CIP catalogue record for this book is available from the British Library.

A & C Black uses paper produced with elemental chlorine-free pulp, harvested from managed sustainable forests.

Printed and bound in Great Britain by Cromwell Press Ltd, Trowbridge.

Introduction

Developing Numeracy: Solving Problems is a series of seven photocopiable activity books designed to be used during the daily maths lesson. They focus on the third strand of the National Numeracy Strategy *Framework for teaching mathematics*. The activities are intended to be used in the time allocated to pupil activities; they aim to reinforce the knowledge, understanding and skills taught during the main part of the lesson and to provide practice and consolidation of the objectives contained in the framework document.

Year R supports the teaching of mathematics by providing a series of activities which develop essential skills in solving mathematical problems. On the whole the activities are designed for children to work on independently, although due to the young age of the children, the teacher may need to read the instructions with the children and ensure that they understand the activity before they begin working on it.

Year R teaches children to:
- recognise and repeat simple patterns;
- solve simple problems and puzzles in practical contexts;
- make simple estimates and predictions;
- sort and match objects, pictures and people;
- use developing mathematical ideas and methods to solve practical problems involving counting and comparing;
- use and understand the vocabulary related to money;
- understand the value of coins and how to use them.

Extension

Many of the activity sheets end with a challenge (**Now try this!**) which reinforces and extends the children's learning, and provides the teacher with the opportunity for assessment. Again, it may be necessary to read the instructions with the children before they begin the activity. For some of the challenges the children will need to record their answers on a separate piece of paper.

Differentiated activities

For some activities, two differentiated versions are provided which have the same title and are presented on facing pages in the book. On the left is the less challenging activity, indicated by a rocket icon: . The more challenging version is found on the right, indicated by a shooting star: . These activity sheets could be given to different groups within the class, or all the children could complete the first sheet and children requiring further extension could then be given the second sheet.

Organisation

Very little equipment is needed, but it will be useful to have available: coloured pencils, interlocking cubes, counters, scissors, glue, dice, coins and number lines. You will need to provide sets of dominoes (0 to double 9) for pages 18 and 19, leaves for page 30, boxes of cubes for page 31 and clock faces for page 34.

To help teachers to select appropriate learning experiences for the children, the activities are grouped into sections within each book. However, the activities are not expected to be used in that order unless otherwise stated. The sheets are intended to support, rather than direct, the teacher's planning.

Some activities can be made easier or more challenging by masking and substituting some of the numbers. You may wish to re-use some pages by copying them onto card and laminating them, or by enlarging them onto A3 paper.

Teachers' notes

Very brief notes are provided at the foot of each page giving ideas and suggestions for maximising the effectiveness of the activity sheets. These can be masked before copying.

Structure of the daily maths lesson

The recommended structure of the daily maths lesson for Key Stage 1 is as follows:

Start to lesson, oral work, mental calculation	5–10 minutes
Main teaching and pupil activities (*the activities in the **Developing Numeracy** books are designed to be carried out in the time allocated to pupil activities*)	about 30 minutes
Plenary (*whole-class review and consolidation*)	about 10 minutes

A reception class may be organised slightly differently:

- an introduction with the whole class which may include finger games, number rhymes and songs;
- some teaching of the whole class on the main maths topic for the day;
- group activities – either all the children divided into small groups working simultaneously on the same area of maths, or groups of children taking part in turn throughout the day in one or more play activities linked to the theme of the lesson, usually supported by an adult.
- a plenary session with the whole class after the group activities are ended to consolidate and extend the children's learning through questions and discussion.

Whole-class activities

The following activities provide some practical ideas which can be used to introduce or reinforce the main teaching part of the lesson.

Recognising patterns

The children could look at and describe fabric, pottery, gift-wrap and wallpaper patterns, and match samples of them. They could also wrap 'presents' and attach matching cards. They could be encouraged to describe the patterns as they point to their repeated elements.

Solving problems and puzzles

The activities in this section could be introduced using real objects, for example, by making sets of ten eggs from Plasticine or dough. The children could arrange them in different ways in and out of a small plastic pot.

They could also select dominoes from a real set whose spots add up to a given number.

Estimating and predicting

The children should have opportunities to estimate quantities, volumes and weight. Help them to check their estimations and provide practice in estimating quantities.

In whole-class and group activities with the teacher, the children could point to where they think a given number will be on a number line which is marked only with lines, on a ruler which is marked only at intervals of ten centimetres and on clock faces marked only with lines or dots for the numerals.

Sorting and matching

To accompany these activities, the children could sort objects in the classroom, for example, ask them to sort a mixture of pencils and felt-tipped pens. They could match objects with the same shape (square, circle, triangle), and discuss the similarities between the shapes they have matched. The children could also play shape-spotting 'I spy' games.

Before the children begin the activities on shapes, discuss and name the shapes: triangle, square, oblong or rectangle, circle, cross, half-circle or semi-circle, diamond, moon (the word 'crescent' could be introduced and the children could look for examples of crescents in pictures and on flags), star, heart, club and spade (as on playing cards). Ask the children to describe the shapes in terms of straight lines, curved lines, corners or points, and anything else they notice.

Some of the activities could be linked with work on mirrors and symmetry: provide a mirror and a collection of halves (just one half) of roughly symmetrical objects such as leaves, coasters, star shapes, and pictures of snowflakes, shells and starfish. Let the children use mirrors to make the whole shape.

Counting and comparing

There are many action rhymes which can help to build children's confidence in counting as they sing or join in with the actions. These include *Five little ducks*, *Three cheeky monkeys*, *There were ten in the bed*, *One, two, buckle my shoe* and *On the first day of Christmas*.

'Real life' and money

To reinforce these activities the children can play 'shop' using real or plastic money. This provides opportunities for the children to make use of their learning about numbers, counting, number operations and money in practical situations.

Tropical fish

- **Colour the odd one out in each bowl.**

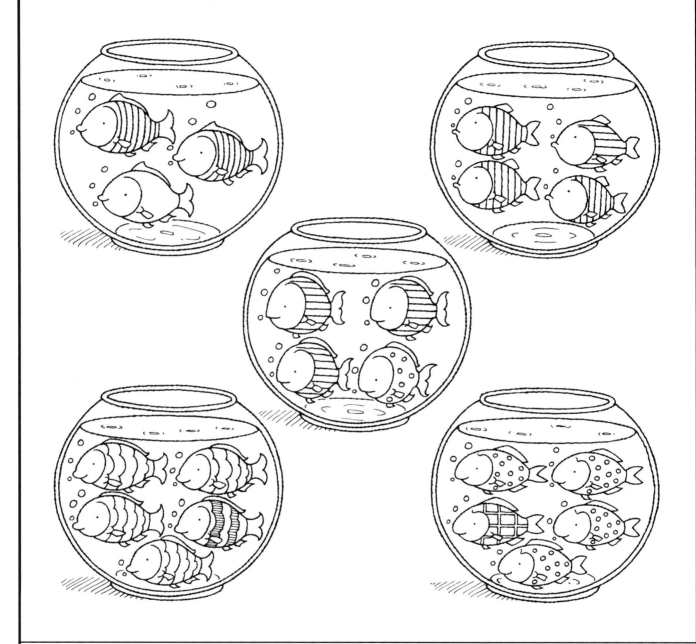

- **Draw the same pattern on 2 fish.**
- **Make the other fish the odd one out.**

Teachers' note Discuss the patterns on the fish. Ask the children to describe the patterns, noticing whether there are lines or spots and, if there are lines, whether they are straight or curved and whether they go across the fish or up and down. For the extension activity, discuss with the children what sort of patterns could be used.

**Developing Numeracy
Solving Problems Year R
© A & C Black**

Elephants

- **Cut out the cards.**

- **Sort the elephants into groups.**

Teachers' note The children could make patterns with different sequences of elephants, or they could rearrange the elephants in groups with one of each kind.

**Developing Numeracy
Solving Problems Year R
© A & C Black**

• **Match the cards to the presents.**

• **Draw a matching pattern on the card and present.**

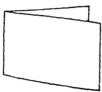

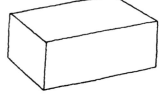

Teachers' note Provide a collection of wrapping paper with matching gift tags. Mix them up for the children to match. They could wrap boxes as 'presents' and fix cards onto them.

Developing Numeracy
Solving Problems Year R
© A & C Black

Broken pots

• **Match the pieces to the pots.**

• **Draw another patterned pot.**

Now try this!

Teachers' note Discuss the patterns on the two pots. Ask the children to describe the patterns on them: are the lines straight or wavy? Ensure that the children understand that they should draw lines to link all four pieces to each pot. For the extension activity, some children might find it easier to trace the pot outline.

Developing Numeracy Solving Problems Year R © A & C Black

9

Patchwork quilt

• **Colour the patches on the quilt.**

red   blue   yellow   green

• **Draw another patchwork quilt.**

Use these patterns.

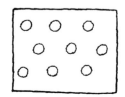 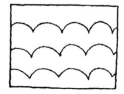 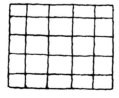 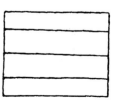

Teachers' note Ask the children to point to patterns which are the same, and to describe them: do they have spots, spirals or lines (and are the lines straight or jagged)? Ensure that they notice the repeating pattern. Link this activity with story books such as *The Patchwork Quilt* (Valerie Flournoy). The children could glue squares of different fabrics onto card in a patchwork pattern.

**Developing Numeracy
Solving Problems Year R
© A & C Black**

Animal parade

- Draw the animal which comes next.   • Write the name of the animal.

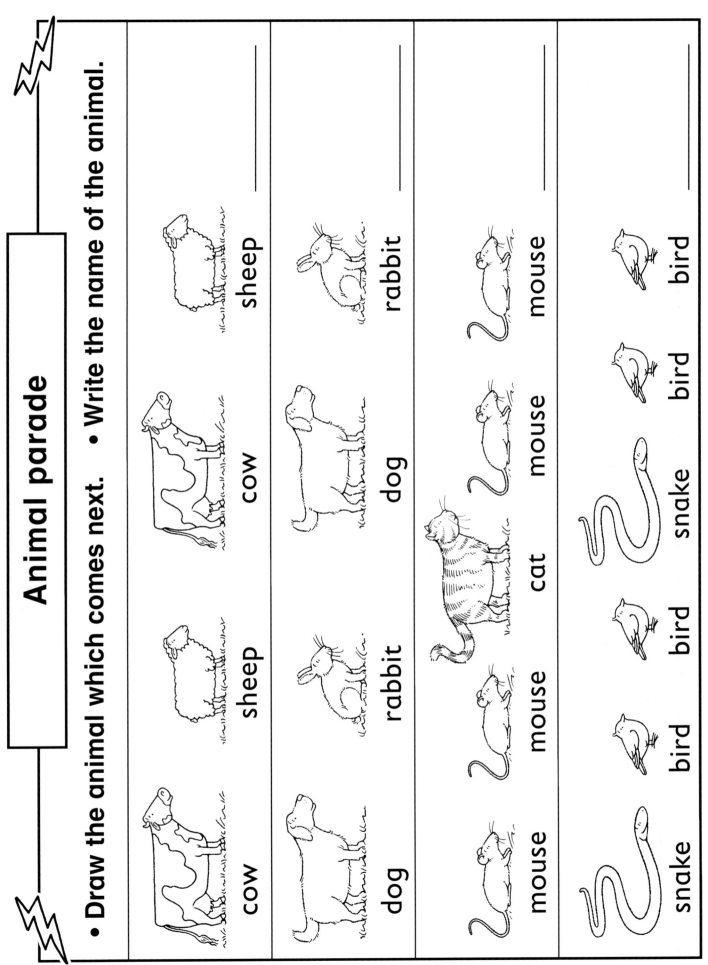

cow	sheep	sheep	
dog	rabbit	rabbit	
mouse	mouse	cat	mouse	mouse
snake	bird	bird	bird	bird	snake

Developing Numeracy
Solving Problems Year R
© A & C Black

Teachers' note If necessary, some children could say the animal names instead of writing them. The children could make their own 'parades' of model animals with repeating patterns.

Shape trains

- Draw the shapes which come next. • Write the names of the shapes.

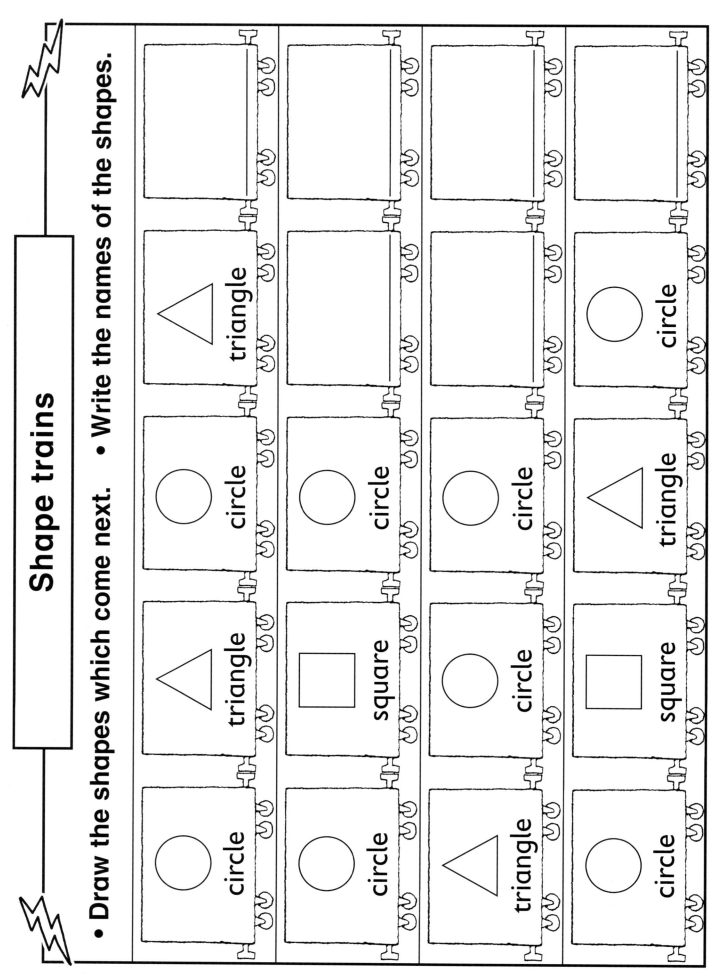

Row 1: circle — triangle — circle — triangle — [blank]

Row 2: circle — square — circle — [blank] — [blank]

Row 3: triangle — circle — circle — [blank] — [blank]

Row 4: circle — square — triangle — circle — [blank]

Teachers' note The shapes and names can be masked before photocopying, and others inserted, to provide a flexible resource. Children could use wooden shapes to make their own repeating patterns.

**Developing Numeracy
Solving Problems Year R
© A & C Black**

Traffic jams

- **Colour the cars.** • **Write the missing colours.**

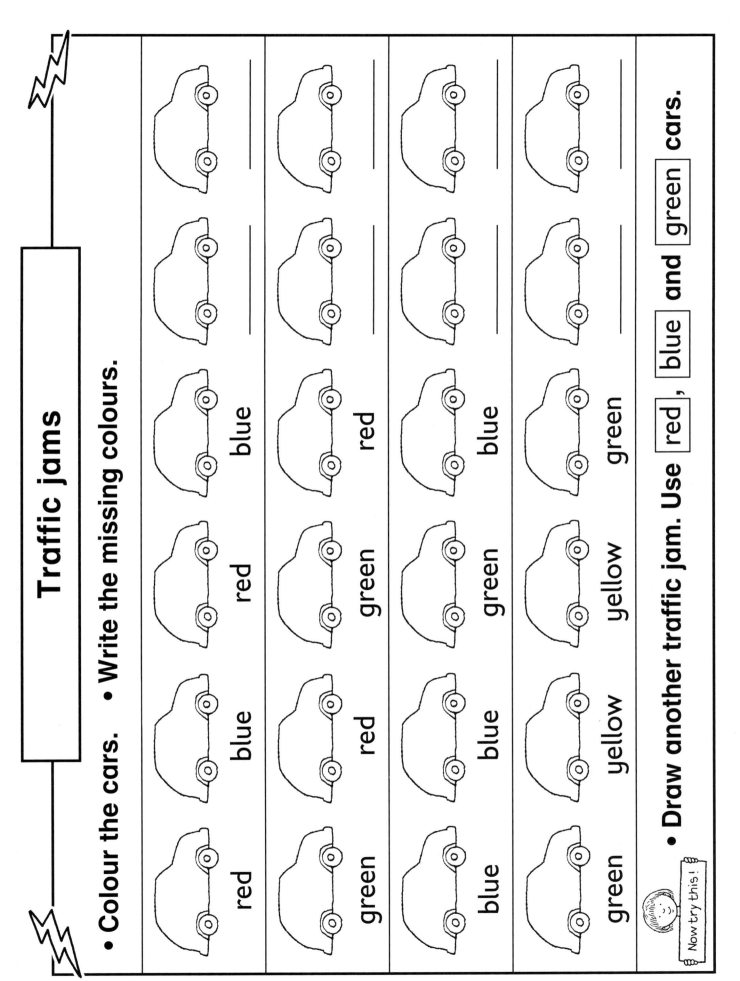

			blue	red	blue
			red	green	red
			green	red	green
			blue	green	blue
			green	yellow	yellow

- **Draw another traffic jam. Use** red , blue **and** green **cars.**

Now try this!

Teachers' note Read the names of the colours with the children and provide a word bank of the names written in the appropriate colour. Encourage the children to say the names of the colours while pointing to the cars and to continue doing so even where there is a gap. They could also make up repeating patterns using toy cars, trucks, vans, and so on.

**Developing Numeracy
Solving Problems Year R**
© A & C Black

13

Fairy lights

- **Colour the lights to make patterns.**

Tell a partner about your pattern.

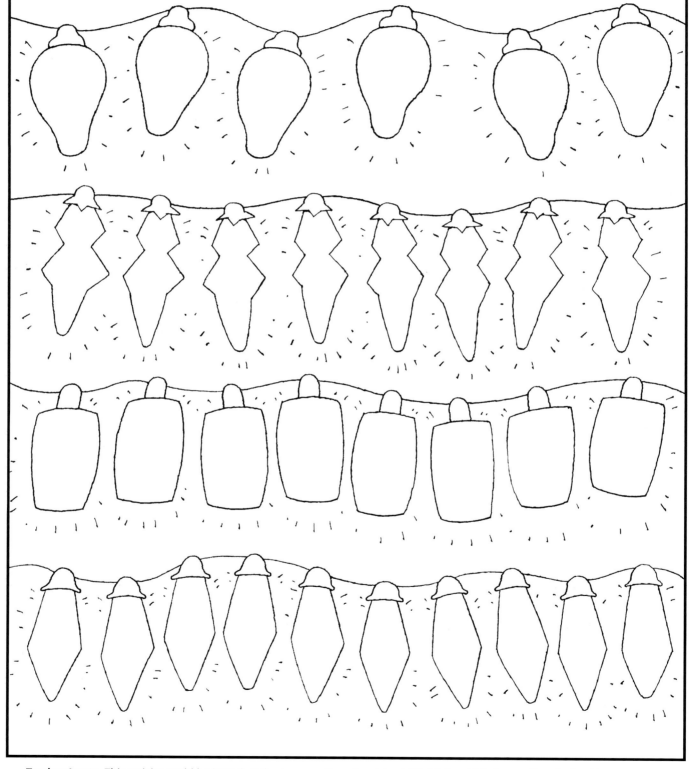

Teachers' note This activity could be introduced using a section of a string of lights in which the colours are arranged in sequence. Point to the lights, naming the colours. The number of colours and lights provided can be varied depending on the children's ability.

**Developing Numeracy
Solving Problems Year R**
© A & C Black

Carnival flags

• Finish the patterns.

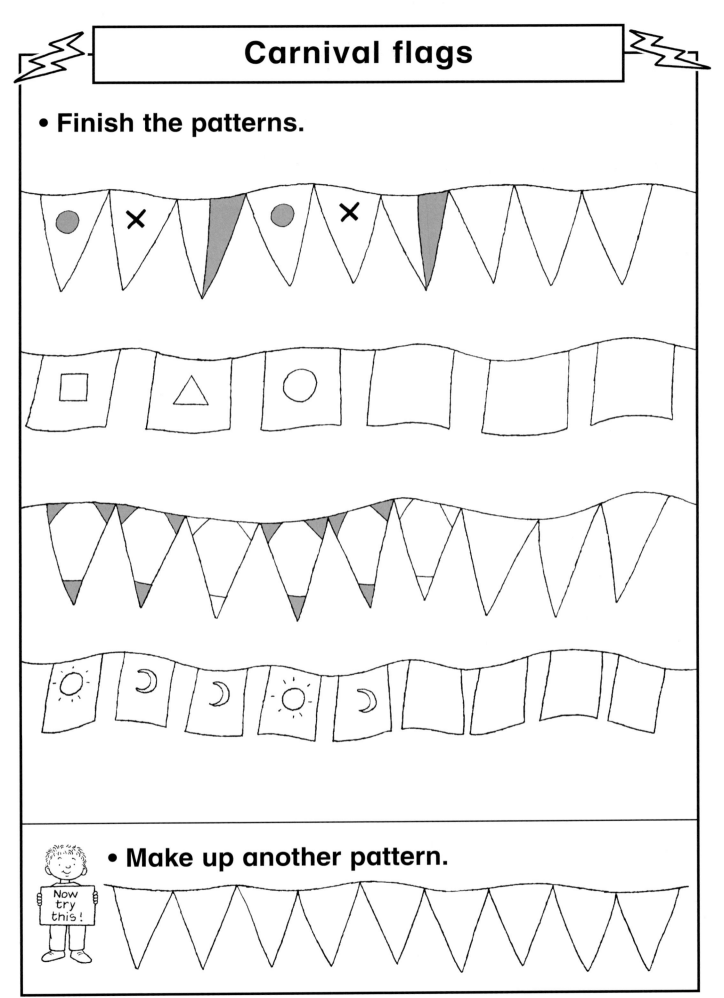

• Make up another pattern.

Teachers' note Encourage the children to describe the patterns as they point to the flags, for example: 'spot, cross, stripe, spot, cross, stripe'. Provide pencils or crayons with fairly fine leads to facilitate the drawing of the small shapes. Copies could be made of real flags, and patterns made from them for the children to complete.

Developing Numeracy
Solving Problems Year R
© A & C Black

Nests

- **Draw some eggs** $\boxed{\text{in}}$ **the nest.**
- **Draw some eggs** $\boxed{\text{out}}$ **of the nest.**
- **Write the numbers.**

Use all the eggs.

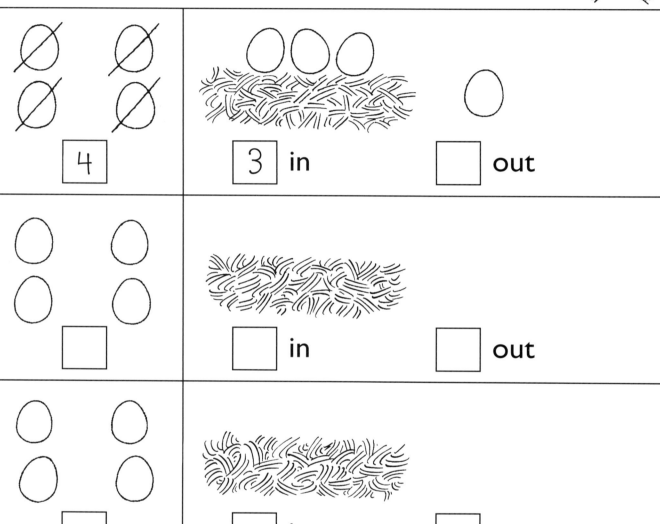

⌀ ⌀ ⌀ ⌀ $\boxed{4}$	🥚🥚🥚 🥚 $\boxed{3}$ in $\boxed{}$ out
🥚 🥚 🥚 🥚 $\boxed{}$	$\boxed{}$ in $\boxed{}$ out
🥚 🥚 🥚 🥚 $\boxed{}$	$\boxed{}$ in $\boxed{}$ out

- **Draw the ways you can put 5 eggs** $\boxed{\text{in}}$ **and** $\boxed{\text{out}}$ **of a nest.**
- **Write the numbers.**

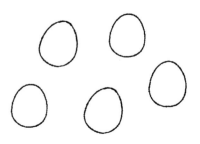

Teachers' note If necessary, revise the words 'in' and 'out'. In each example, all the eggs should be used; encourage the children to cross out each egg as they draw it in the nest or out of the nest. The children should make a different combination each time.

**Developing Numeracy
Solving Problems Year R
© A & C Black**

16

Nests

- **Draw some eggs** | in | **the nest.**
- **Draw some eggs** | out | **of the nest.**
- **Write the numbers.**

> Use all the eggs.

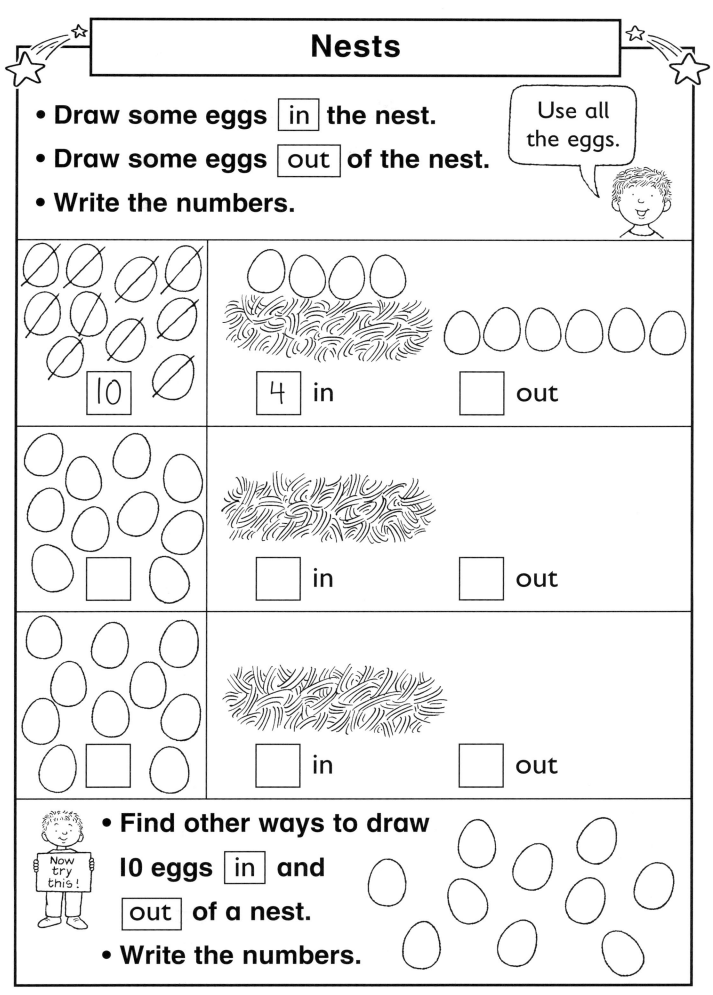

10

4 in [ ] out

[ ] in [ ] out

[ ] in [ ] out

- **Find other ways to draw 10 eggs** | in | **and** | out | **of a nest.**
- **Write the numbers.**

Now try this!

Teachers' note This activity can be used as an extension of the previous page. It can also be used in conjunction with work on 'making 10'. The children should make a different combination each time.

**Developing Numeracy
Solving Problems Year R
© A & C Black**

Domino spots

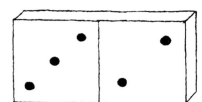

This domino has a total of $\boxed{5}$ spots.

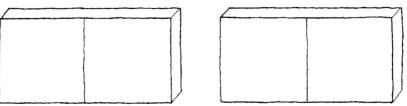

- Draw 2 other dominoes with a total of $\boxed{5}$ spots.

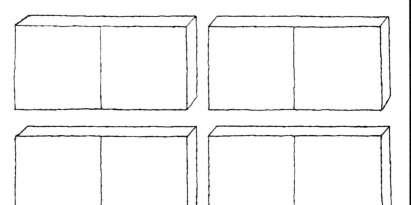

- Find all the dominoes with a total of $\boxed{6}$ spots.
- Draw the spots.

- Find all the dominoes with a total of $\boxed{7}$ spots.
- Draw the spots.

- How many dominoes do you think have a total of $\boxed{8}$ spots? ☐
- Draw the dominoes.

Teachers' note Use a set of dominoes up to double 9. The children could also find as many different ways as possible of making a total of 5, 6 and 7 using two dice.

Developing Numeracy
Solving Problems Year R
© A & C Black

Domino spots

This domino has a total

of ☐10☐ spots.

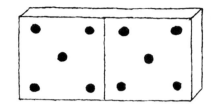

• **Draw 4 other dominoes with a total of** ☐10☐ **spots.**

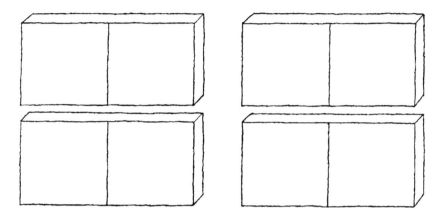

• **How many dominoes do you think**

have a total of ☐12☐ **spots?** ☐

• **Draw the dominoes.**

• **Do you think there will be more dominoes**

with ☐13☐ **spots or with** ☐14☐ **spots? Or will**

there be the same number? Find out.

Teachers' note Use a set of dominoes up to double 9. The children should first complete the activity on page 18. Ask the children what they notice about the numbers of dominoes which have totals of 12 and 13 spots. They might be surprised to find that a higher number does not necessarily have more combinations of spots.

Developing Numeracy
Solving Problems Year R
© A & C Black

Cars

- **Cut out the cards.**
- **Make a pattern with some of the cards.**
- **Glue them onto a piece of paper.**

Teachers' note For this activity, give the children a piece of paper on which is drawn a line to represent a road. Ask them to arrange a given number of between four and six cars along the 'road' in a repeating pattern. Then ask them what they can try next. This activity could be introduced using toy cars.

**Developing Numeracy
Solving Problems Year R**
© A & C Black

Fruit bowls

- **Draw the fruit in the bowls.**
- **Write the numbers to total** $\boxed{6}$.

 Use all the fruit.

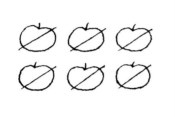

$\boxed{2}$ + $\boxed{4}$ → $\boxed{6}$

$\square$ + $\square$ → $\square$

$\square$ + $\square$ → $\square$

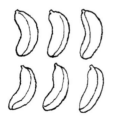

$\square$ + $\square$ → $\square$

- **Find ways to put** $\boxed{8}$ **oranges in 2 bowls.**
- **Write the numbers.**

Teachers' note To keep track of the fruit they have used, the children should cross out each piece of fruit as they draw it in a bowl. If necessary, revise 'zero'. Encourage the children to say what they are doing, for example: 'two in here and four in here'. The children should find a different way to arrange the fruit each time. This activity could be introduced practically.

Developing Numeracy
Solving Problems Year R
© A & C Black

Apples

- **Colour the apples as long as each branch.**

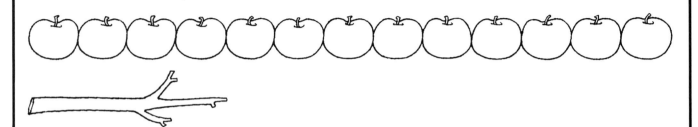

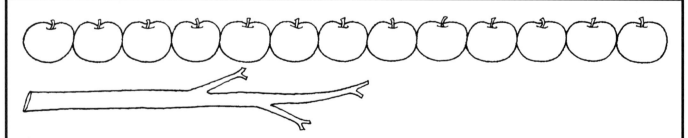

- **Draw another branch.**
- **Draw a line of apples as long as the branch.**

Teachers' note Before the children colour the apples, ask them to point out each end of the branch and the first and last apple they will colour in the line. They could make up some examples of their own with longer branches. They need not count the apples; the purpose of the activity is for them to match lengths.

**Developing Numeracy
Solving Problems Year R
© A & C Black**

• **Colour the blocks as tall as each toy.**

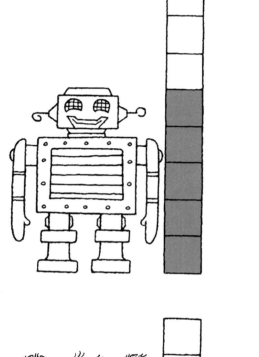
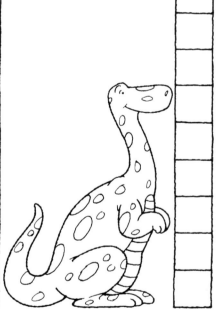

• **Choose your own toy.**

• **Make a tower of blocks as tall as the toy.**

Teachers' note For the extension activity, the children should use either interlocking cubes or large blocks which are not too difficult to balance. They need not count the blocks; the purpose of the activity is for them to match heights.

**Developing Numeracy
Solving Problems Year R
© A & C Black**

Picture puzzle

- ## Cut out the pieces.
- ## Make the picture.

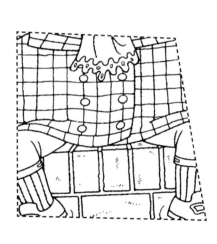

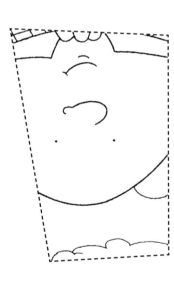

Teachers' note The children could work with a partner. Encourage them to discuss the way in which they are solving the puzzle, for example: 'I have found the bottom part of Humpty's body, I need the part with his eyes'; 'All these pieces have parts of the wall, so they must join one another'. They could cut up greetings cards for a partner to put together.

**Developing Numeracy
Solving Problems Year R
© A & C Black**

- **Find the missing piece from each cake.**

- **Copy it in the space.**

- **Fill in the pattern on this cake.**

Teachers' note Cut quarters out of other circular shapes such as decorated paper plates. Mix them up and ask the children to fit the pieces into the correct plate.

**Developing Numeracy
Solving Problems Year R
© A & C Black**

Necklaces

• **Draw the missing beads.**

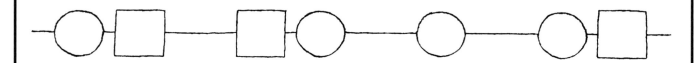

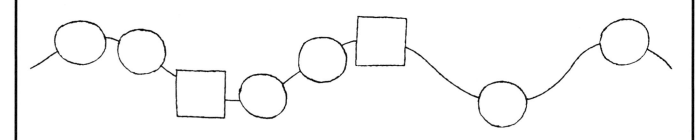

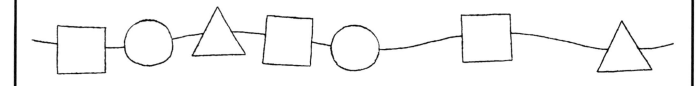

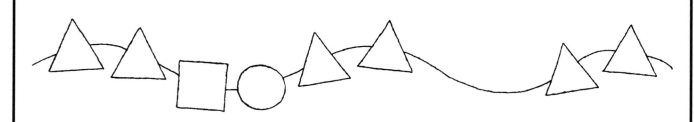

 • **Make another necklace. Use**  ☐ , △ **and** ◯ **.**

Teachers' note The children should first make sequences of different kinds and say the word for each sound, action, shape or number as they come to it in the sequence, for example: 'Clap, stamp, clap, stamp'. In this activity, ask the children to say the names of the shapes as they point to them and as they come to the gaps. Ask them to repeat this to check their answers.

**Developing Numeracy
Solving Problems Year R
© A & C Black**

Hide and seek

• **What number will each child say next?**

1, 2, 3, ____

6, 7, 8, ____

5, 6, 7, ____

3, 4, 5, ____

4, 5, 6, ____

7, 8, 9, ____

• **Write the missing numbers.**

5, 6, ____ , 8, 9, ____

9, 10, ____ , ____ , 13

Teachers' note Encourage the children to read aloud the numbers in the sequences and to repeat this after completing them. A partner could help them to check their answers. They should have regular practice of number sequences.

Developing Numeracy
Solving Problems Year R
© A & C Black

- **Write the missing numbers.**

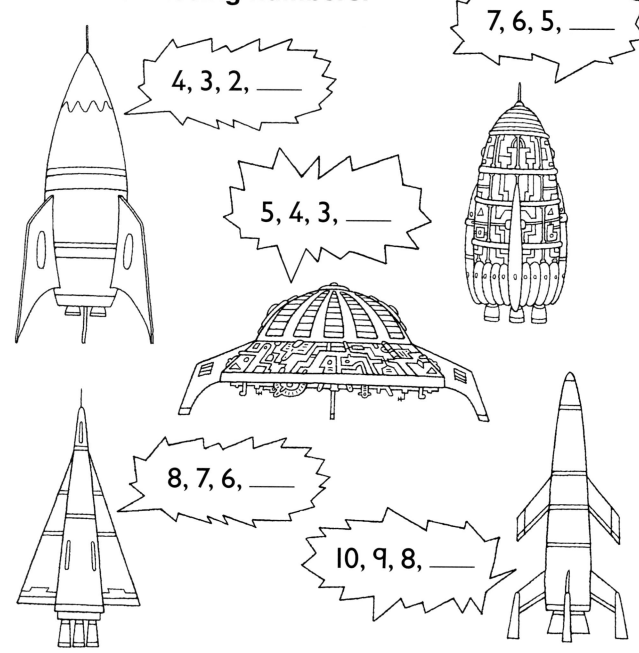

7, 6, 5, ____

4, 3, 2, ____

5, 4, 3, ____

8, 7, 6, ____

10, 9, 8, ____

Now try this!

- **Write the missing numbers.**

10, ____ , 8, 7, 6, ____ , 4

12, ____ , 10, 9, ____ , 7

13, ____ , 11, 10, ____ , ____

Teachers' note The children need to practise counting backwards, first from five to zero and then from ten to zero. This could be linked with role-play in which they launch 'spacecraft' counting back from ten to 'Blast off!'. Encourage them to listen to each other, to spot any numbers they miss. Also practise counting-down rhymes, for example: *Ten green bottles*.

Developing Numeracy Solving Problems Year R © A & C Black

Cat and mouse

• **Which things can the mouse hide in?** ✓ or ✗

• **Draw 2 other things for the mouse to hide in.**

Teachers' note This could be introduced using a 'mouse' toy and a set of objects in which the mouse may try to hide. Hold up an object and ask, 'Can the mouse hide in here?'. Then ask the children to check. A mouse could be cut out from a spare copy of this sheet for the children to check their answers to this page.

**Developing Numeracy
Solving Problems Year R
© A & C Black**

29

Ladybirds

- Estimate how many ladybirds will fit along each leaf. ☐ • Check. ☐

3
3

You need 3 real leaves.

- Estimate how many ladybirds will fit along them.
- Check.

Teachers' note After the children have estimated how many ladybirds will fit along each leaf, cut out the strip of ladybirds on the right-hand side of the page so that the children can check their answers.

Developing Numeracy
Solving Problems Year R
© A & C Black

Dogs and bones

- **Are there enough bones for the dogs?**
- **Estimate.** yes or no • **Check.** ✓ or ✗

	yes
	✓

You need a box of cubes.

- **Are there enough cubes for the whole group to have one?**
- **Estimate.** ☐ • **Check.** ☐

Now try this!

Teachers' note Ask the children to estimate by looking at the pictures, and not by counting. They can check their answers by drawing lines to match each dog to a bone or by counting them and comparing the numbers. Ensure that the children understand the term 'enough'. The estimating in the extension activity can be done individually and then checked as a group.

**Developing Numeracy
Solving Problems Year R
© A & C Black**

Circus clowns

- **Are there enough hats for the clowns?**
- **Estimate.** ☑   • **Check.** yes or no

just enough ☐
too few ☐
too many ✓

yes

just enough ☐
too few ☐
too many ☐

☐

just enough ☐
too few ☐
too many ☐

☐

just enough ☐
too few ☐
too many ☐

☐

Now try this!

- **Draw some clowns.**
- **Your partner draws some hats.**
- **Look at the pictures. Are there**

just enough **hats,** too few **or** too many **?**

Teachers' note Ask the children to estimate by looking at the pictures, and not by counting. They can check their answers by crossing out a clown and a hat as they are matched. Some children might then be able to count the hats and clowns and compare the numbers. Ensure that the children understand the terms 'just enough', 'too few' and 'too many'.

Developing Numeracy
Solving Problems Year R
© A & C Black

At the bus station

- **Estimate.**

  Write in pencil.

- **Then check.**

  Write in pen.

- **Find** 5 **. Write 5 on the correct bus.**

| 1 | 2 | | 4 | | 6 | 7 | 8 |

- **Find** 6 **.**

| 3 | 4 | | | | | | 10 |

- **Find** 4 **.**

| 2 | | | | | 7 | 8 | 9 |

- **Find** 8 **.**

| 3 | | | 6 | | | | 10 |

Now try this!

- **Fill in the missing numbers.**

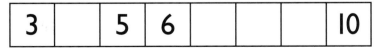

| 3 | | 5 | 6 | | | 10 |

- **Use counters to cover 2 numbers.**

- **Ask a partner which they are.**

Take turns.

Teachers' note Ask the children to estimate by pointing to the place where the number should be, and not by counting. They write the number in pencil, then check by counting; they write the checked number in pen.

**Developing Numeracy
Solving Problems Year R
© A & C Black**

Clocks

- **Estimate.**

  Write in pencil.

- **Then check.**

  Write in pen.

- **Find** 3 **and** 6 .

- **Find** 5 **and** 9 .

- **Find** 1 **and** 7 .

- **Find** 4 **and** 11 .

- **Cover some of the numbers on a clock face.**
- **Choose a number for a friend to find.**
- **Check your friend's answer.**

Teachers' note Ask the children to estimate by pointing to the place where the number should be, and not by counting. They write the number in pencil, and then check by counting; they write the checked number in pen. For the extension activity, provide the children with a clock face and counters with which to cover the numbers.

**Developing Numeracy
Solving Problems Year R
© A & C Black**

Where does it belong? Places

purse

jewellery box

pencil box

vase

Teachers' note Use this with page 36. Cut out the four containers and give one to each child in a group of four. Before beginning the activity, provide opportunities for the children to sort everyday objects into appropriate containers, for example, cutlery into a cutlery tray.

**Developing Numeracy
Solving Problems Year R
© A & C Black**

35

Where does it belong? Objects

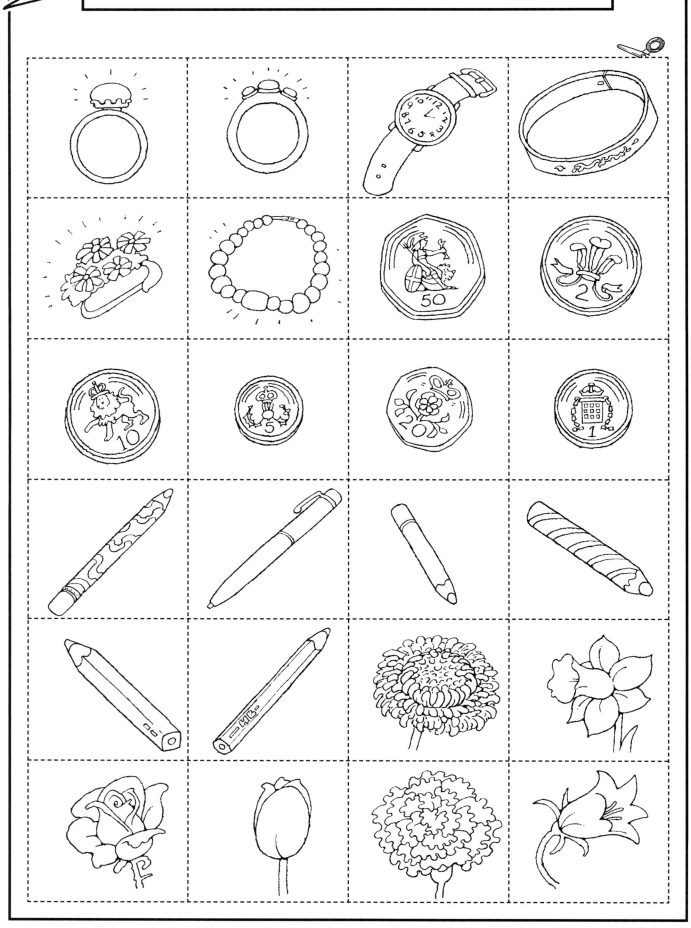

Teachers' note Use this with page 35. Cut out the picture cards and place them face down. The children take turns to turn over a card. If it belongs in their container, they keep it; if not, they turn it back. The winner is the first to collect all six objects for his or her container.

**Developing Numeracy
Solving Problems Year R**
© A & C Black

Shape match

- **Colour the shapes which are the same.**

- **Use a different colour for each shape.**

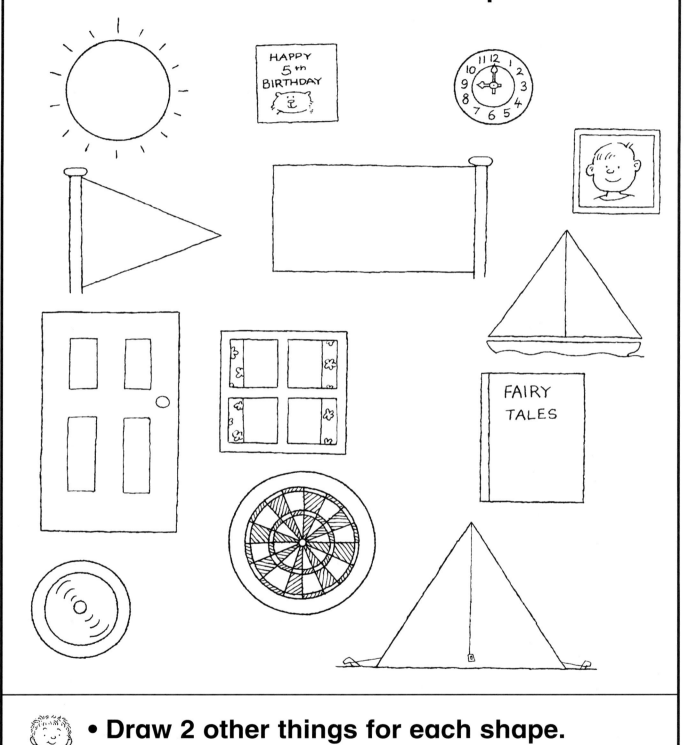

- **Draw 2 other things for each shape.**

Teachers' note The children should colour the shapes which have the same characteristics. As an introduction, they may need practice in recognising characteristics of shapes (see page 5). You could provide magazines and brochures from which the children can cut pictures of objects with the shapes shown. Ask them to label the shapes 'square', 'rectangle', 'circle' and 'triangle'.

**Developing Numeracy
Solving Problems Year R
© A & C Black**

Shape pairs

Teachers' note Cut out the shape cards and turn them face down. In a group, the children take turns to turn over two cards. If they are the same, they keep them; if not, they turn them back. Encourage them to try to remember the whereabouts of the shapes they have seen. The cards can also be used for playing 'Snap'. You may wish to discuss the names of the shapes (see page 5).

**Developing Numeracy
Solving Problems Year R
© A & C Black**

Wheel puzzle

• **Draw lines to match the halves.**

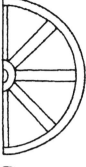

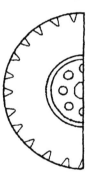
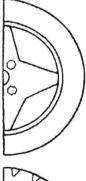

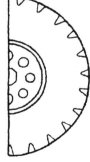

• **Draw 4 other wheels.**

• **Cut them in half for a partner to match.**

Find a circle to draw round.

Teachers' note The children can check their answers by cutting out and matching the halves of the wheels.

Developing Numeracy
Solving Problems Year R
© A & C Black

Shape sorting

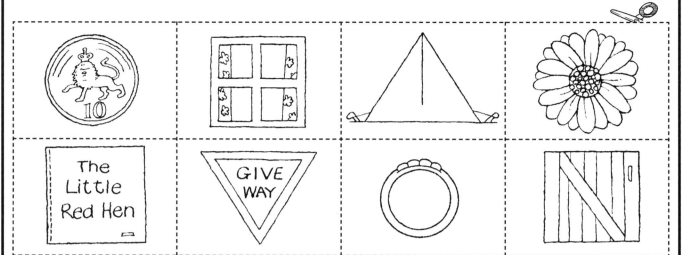

- **Cut out the picture cards.**
- **Glue them on the chart.**

squares ☐	circles ○	triangles △

- **Make another chart.**
- **Draw pictures on it using ☐ , ○ and △ .**

Teachers' note The children could describe how they recognise each shape. For the extension activity, they could look in books and magazines, as well as at real objects, for items to copy.

**Developing Numeracy
Solving Problems Year R
© A & C Black**

Find the shape

• **Colour the shape which goes with each set.**

shape	set

• **Draw another shape in each set.**

Now try this!

Teachers' note The children should look for similarities between two-dimensional shapes, for example, whether or not the shapes have any straight sides or any curved sides. They are not expected to know the names of all the shapes, although these can be introduced if desired.

**Developing Numeracy
Solving Problems Year R
© A & C Black**

Animal allsorts

- **Cut out the cards.**
- **Sort the animals into sets.**
- **Explain to a partner how you sorted them.**

Example:

These have no legs.

Teachers' note The children sort the animals according to criteria of their choice, for example: legs/no legs, wings/no wings, shell/no shell, fur/no fur, scales/no scales. Some children might be able to sort the animals according to the number of legs: 0, 2, 4 or 6. This could be linked with work in science on the classification of animals according to observable features.

**Developing Numeracy
Solving Problems Year R
© A & C Black**

Robots

- **Cut out the cards.**

- **Sort the robots into families.**

Teachers' note The children should arrange the robots in groups of the same kind. Encourage them to notice the shapes of the heads, bodies and limbs; the number of legs; the shape of the eyes. The children could also arrange all or a selection of the robots in a line from small to large.

**Developing Numeracy
Solving Problems Year R
© A & C Black**

Sock mix-up

Are there enough socks for the children?

• Write ┌yes┐ or ┌no┐ .

 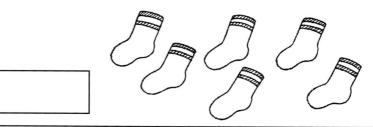

 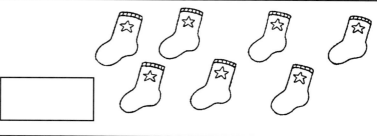

 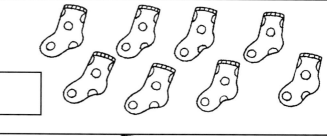

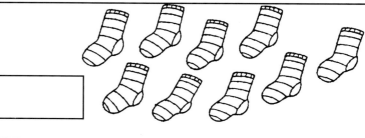

• **Draw 6 children.**

• **Draw enough socks for them.**

Teachers' note The children count to find the answers; they could work out the solutions by counting the socks in twos. Ensure that the children understand the term 'enough'.

**Developing Numeracy
Solving Problems Year R
© A & C Black**

Building blocks

- **Look at the children's plans.**

- **How many more blocks of each kind do they need?**

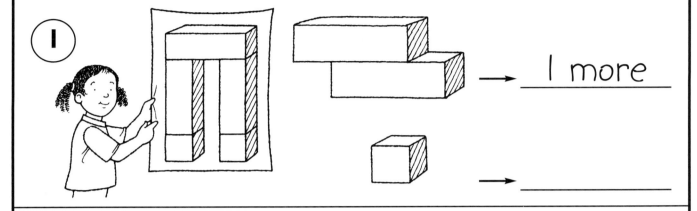

① → _I more_

→ _____

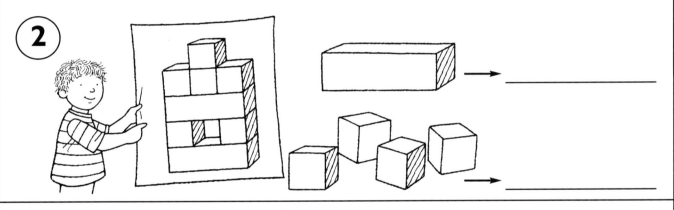

② → _____

→ _____

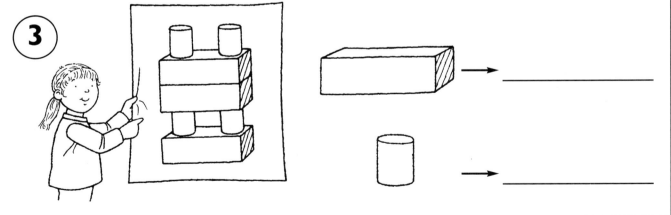

③ → _____

→ _____

- **Which plan has the** [most] **blocks?** ◯

- **Which plan has the** [fewest] **blocks?** ◯

Teachers' note To introduce or reinforce the activity, the children could build a simple structure from different kinds of blocks and record the numbers of each kind of block. Ensure that the children understand the terms 'more', 'most' and 'fewest'.

Developing Numeracy
Solving Problems Year R
© A & C Black

Breakfast stories

1	2	3	4	5	6	7	8	9	10
one	two	three	four	five	six	seven	eight	nine	ten

- **Write how many eggs.**

Two eggs, please.

Two eggs, please.

4 eggs

Two eggs, please.

One egg, please.

Two eggs, please.

☐ eggs

No eggs, thank you.

Three eggs, please.

Two eggs, please.

☐ eggs

Two eggs, please.

Two eggs, please.

Two eggs, please.

☐ eggs

Now try this!

- **Ask your group how many eggs they want.**
- **Write the total.** ☐

Teachers' note The children might find the solutions by counting on, or by using counters to represent the eggs. Ask them to explain the method they used.

**Developing Numeracy
Solving Problems Year R
© A & C Black**

Choosing biscuits

• Choose biscuits from the plates.

You can have
⬚3⬚ biscuits.  ⬚2⬚ and 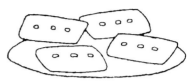 ⬚1⬚

You can have
⬚4⬚ biscuits.  ⬚ ⬚ and  ⬚ ⬚

You can have
⬚5⬚ biscuits.  ⬚ ⬚ and 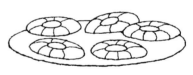 ⬚ ⬚

You can have
⬚6⬚ biscuits. 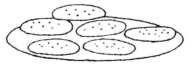 ⬚ ⬚ and  ⬚ ⬚

 You can have ⬚6⬚ biscuits.

• Choose biscuits from any 3 plates.

• Draw the biscuits.

Teachers' note The children should realise that they can take from the first plate either the total number of biscuits or fewer. Ask them to explain how they worked out how many they could take from the second plate. Some children might find it helpful to colour the chosen biscuits and cross out the others.

**Developing Numeracy
Solving Problems Year R
© A & C Black**

Stamps

- **Draw a stamp on each letter.**

- **How many stamps are left?**

3 stamps left

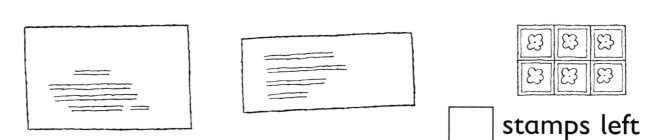

☐ stamps left

☐ stamps left

☐ stamp left

- **Draw 10 stamps.**

- **Draw 4 letters and put a stamp on each.**

- **How many stamps are left?** ☐

Teachers' note The children could first carry out practical examples of distributing given numbers of stamps to letters in a role-play 'post office' using old envelopes and 'stamps' made by cutting perforations in sheets of gummed paper.

Developing Numeracy
Solving Problems Year R
© A & C Black

You need $\boxed{2}$ slices of bread to make a sandwich.

- Write how many slices of bread these children need.

 $\boxed{4}$ slices

 $\boxed{}$ slices

 $\boxed{}$ slices

 $\boxed{}$ slices

- Draw a sandwich for everyone in your group.
- How many slices of bread? $\boxed{}$

Teachers' note The children should explain how they reached their solutions. They might multiply by two, count in twos or use their knowledge of 'doubles' (double 2 = 4, double 3 = 6, and so on).

**Developing Numeracy
Solving Problems Year R
© A & C Black**

Sweet sale

All the sweets are ⟨half price⟩.

- Write the new prices.

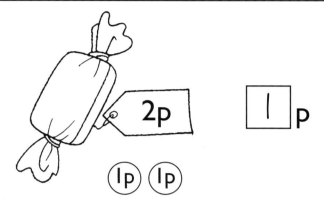

2p   [1]p

(1p) (1p)

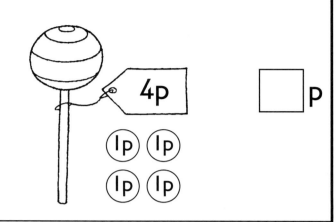

4p   [ ]p

(1p) (1p)
(1p) (1p)

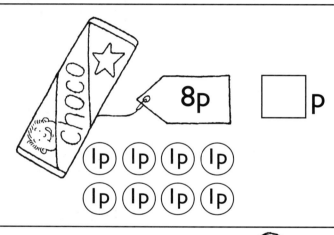

8p   [ ]p

(1p) (1p) (1p) (1p)
(1p) (1p) (1p) (1p)

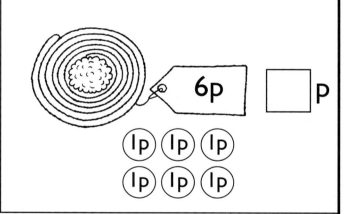

6p   [ ]p

(1p) (1p) (1p)
(1p) (1p) (1p)

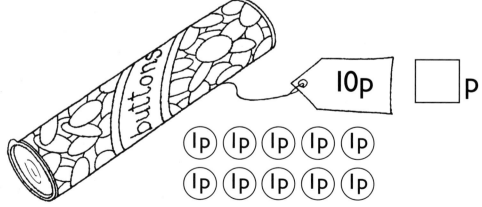

10p   [ ]p

(1p) (1p) (1p) (1p) (1p)
(1p) (1p) (1p) (1p) (1p)

Now try this!

- Draw sweets which cost ⟨12p⟩, ⟨16p⟩ and ⟨14p⟩.
- Write the new prices.

Teachers' note This could be used to consolidate work on twos and doubles. The coins are arranged so that the children can, if they wish, draw a line which splits the total in half. Provide plastic coins and ask the children to find half the total.

Developing Numeracy
Solving Problems Year R
© A & C Black

Find a partner

- **Count the children.**
- **How many pairs?**
- **How many left over?**

3	children
1	pair
1	left over

	children
	pairs
	left over

	children
	pairs
	left over

	children
	pairs
	left over

- **Draw 11 children.**
- **How many pairs?**

	pairs
	left over

Now try this!

Teachers' note This activity could be used to introduce odd and even numbers. Although these terms are not used on the activity sheet, they can be introduced if the children are ready for them. To make pairs, the children should draw a loop around each pair of children. Ask the group what is the greatest number of children there can be left over, and why.

**Developing Numeracy
Solving Problems Year R
© A & C Black**

Birthday cakes

Each cake needs $\boxed{3}$ candles.

- Are there enough candles for the cakes?
- Write $\boxed{\text{yes}}$ or $\boxed{\text{no}}$.

| | | | yes |

| | | | |

| | | | |

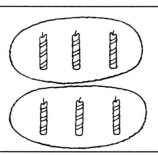

- Draw 10 candles.
- Are there enough for these cakes?

| | | | | | |

Teachers' note The children could draw a loop around each set of three candles and count to check that there is a set for each cake. Ensure that the children understand the term 'enough'. Provide practise in counting sets of three, for example, bears, billy goats gruff and little pigs.

Developing Numeracy
Solving Problems Year R
© A & C Black

Making buggies

Each buggy needs $\boxed{4}$ wheels.

- **Are there enough wheels for the buggies?**
- **Write** $\boxed{\text{yes}}$ **or** $\boxed{\text{no}}$.

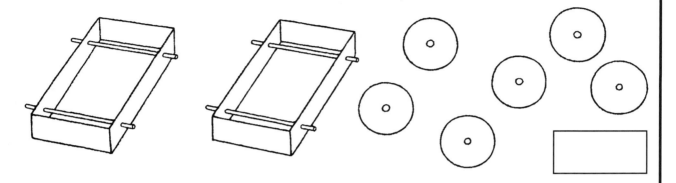

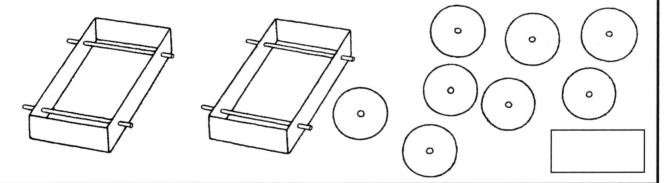

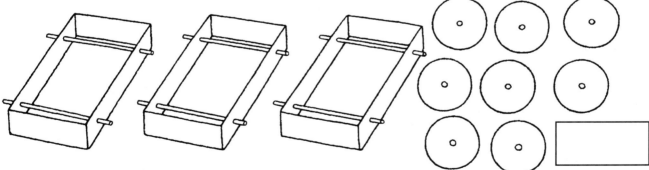

You have 10 wheels.

- **Are there enough for**

2 buggies?

3 buggies?

4 buggies?

Teachers' note Ask the children to explain how they solved the problems. They could draw a loop around each set of four wheels and count to check that there is a set for each buggy. Ensure that the children understand the term 'enough'.

**Developing Numeracy
Solving Problems Year R
© A & C Black**

53

Coin machines

- **Match the coins to the machines.**

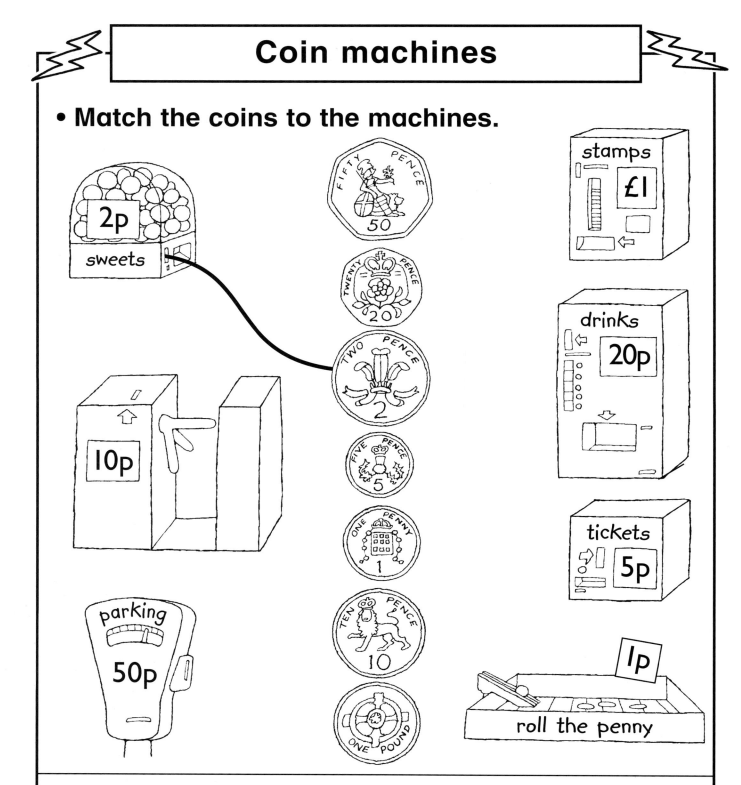

- **Write a price on each machine.**
- **Draw the coins.**

Now try this!

P a ride

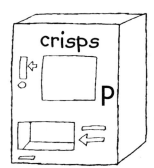

crisps

P

Teachers' note The children could be asked to notice coin machines which they see when they are out and about and to notice the amounts of money which are put into ticket machines, parking meters, vending machines and lockers.

**Developing Numeracy
Solving Problems Year R
© A & C Black**

10p wins

Teachers' note The children need 1p and 2p coins, a die and counters. They throw the die, move their counter and follow the instructions on which they land, taking or replacing coins until they have enough to exchange for a 10p piece. The winner is the first to exchange ten pennies for a 10p piece. Ensure that the children understand the terms 'pay', 'less', 'more' and 'total'.

Developing Numeracy
Solving Problems Year R
© A & C Black

55

Best buys

• **Colour the** cheaper **sweet.**

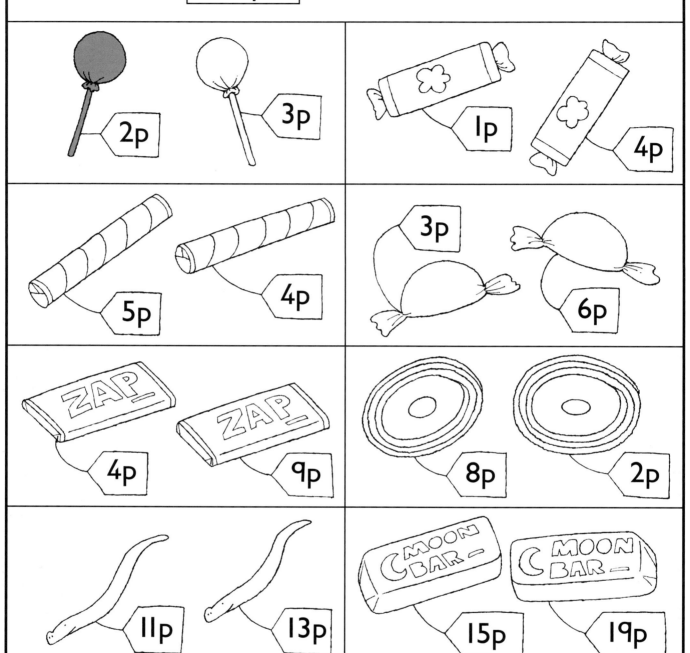

• **Draw 3 sweets.**

• **Write their prices.**

• **Now draw the sweets in order.**

Start with the cheapest .

Teachers' note Before beginning this activity, the children could compare the prices of pairs of items in a class shop. Some of them might be able to say by how much the item is cheaper. Ensure that the children understand the terms 'cheaper' and 'cheapest'.

Developing Numeracy Solving Problems Year R © A & C Black

Toy stall

- **Is there enough money to buy the toy?**
- **Write** yes **or** no .

£2   no

£1

£2

£1 £1

£3

£1 £1 £1 £1

£1

£1 £1 £1

£7

£1 £1 £1 £1 £1

£6

- **If there is not enough money, draw the extra coins you need in the piggy bank.**

Teachers' note Ensure that the children understand the term 'enough'. In the extension activity, the children may need to use real or plastic coins.

Developing Numeracy Solving Problems Year R © A & C Black

Money stories

- **Read the stories.**
- **Write them using numbers.**

Kim has ten pence.

She spends six pence.

change

$\boxed{10}$ p – $\boxed{6}$ p = $\boxed{4}$ p

Bip has five pence.

He spends four pence.

change

$\boxed{}$ p – $\boxed{}$ p = $\boxed{}$ p

Meg has six pence.

She spends five pence.

change

$\boxed{}$ p – $\boxed{}$ p = $\boxed{}$ p

Tom has nine pence.

He spends seven pence.

change

$\boxed{}$ p – $\boxed{}$ p = $\boxed{}$ p

Teachers' note The children could act out money stories, then write them using mathematical notation.

**Developing Numeracy
Solving Problems Year R
© A & C Black**

Money stories

- **Finish the stories.**
- **Write them using numbers.**

Carl has five pence.

He spends two pence.

He gets ⟨ three ⟩

pence change.

| 5 |p − | 2 |p = | 3 |p

Ruby has six pence.

She spends four pence.

She gets ⟨　　⟩

pence change.

| |p − | |p = | |p

Raj has ten pence.

He spends seven pence.

He gets ⟨　　⟩

pence change.

| |p − | |p = | |p

Fay has eight pence.

She spends four pence.

She gets ⟨　　⟩

pence change.

| |p − | |p = | |p

Teachers' note The children could act out money stories, then write them using mathematical notation.

**Developing Numeracy
Solving Problems Year R
© A & C Black**

Teddy bears' picnic

- **Write how much each bear spends.**

$\boxed{2}$ p + $\boxed{6}$ p = $\boxed{8}$ p

$\boxed{}$ p + $\boxed{}$ p = $\boxed{}$ p

$\boxed{}$ p + $\boxed{}$ p = $\boxed{}$ p

$\boxed{}$ p + $\boxed{}$ p = $\boxed{}$ p

$\boxed{}$ p + $\boxed{}$ p = $\boxed{}$ p

$\boxed{}$ p + $\boxed{}$ p = $\boxed{}$ p

- **Draw 2 other bears with picnic food.**
- **Write the prices.**
- **Add them up.**

Teachers' note In the extension activity, the children may need to use real or plastic coins.

Developing Numeracy
Solving Problems Year R
© A & C Black

60

Teddy bears' treasure hunt

- **Write how many hidden pence.** [ ] p
- **Write how many hidden pounds.** £ [ ]

- **The bears want [10p] . How many more pence do they need?** [ ] p
- **The bears want [£10] . How many more pounds do they need?** £ [ ]

Teachers' note Ask the children to think of a way to make sure that they do not count any coins more than once. (They could cross them out or colour them.) Some children might be able to work out the total in pounds and pence.

Developing Numeracy
Solving Problems Year R
© A & C Black

61

The fruit stall

- **Read the price list.**
- **Write the price tags.**
  Use numbers.

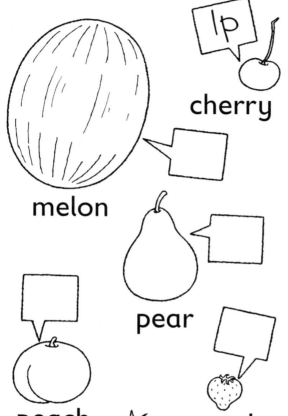

cherry

melon

pear

peach

strawberry

Price list

cherry	–	one penny
grapes	–	nine pence
lemon	–	two pence
melon	–	four pence
peach	–	seven pence
pear	–	three pence
pineapple	–	ten pence
plum	–	five pence
banana	–	eight pence
strawberry	–	six pence

banana

pineapple

grapes

lemon

plum

- **Draw 2 fruits which each cost more than ten pence.**
- **Write the price tags.**

Now try this!

Teachers' note The children could also use a price list to write price labels for items in a class shop. The extension activity provides an opportunity to work with higher numbers for those children who are able.

**Developing Numeracy
Solving Problems Year R
© A & C Black**

Money match: purses

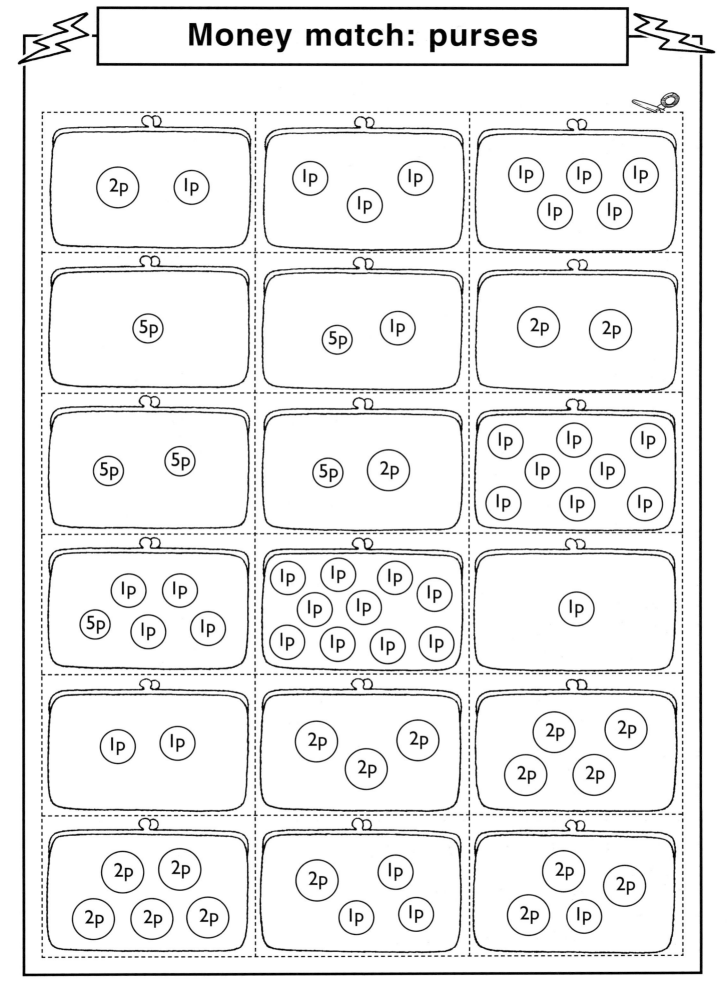

Teachers' note Use this with page 64. It is a matching game which also involves counting and addition. Cut out the 'purse' cards and the 'shopping' cards (page 64). Spread them face down on a table, keeping the two types of cards in separate sets. It may help some children if they add up each total and write it on the card before the game begins. (Continued on page 64.)

Developing Numeracy
Solving Problems Year R
© A & C Black

Money match: shopping

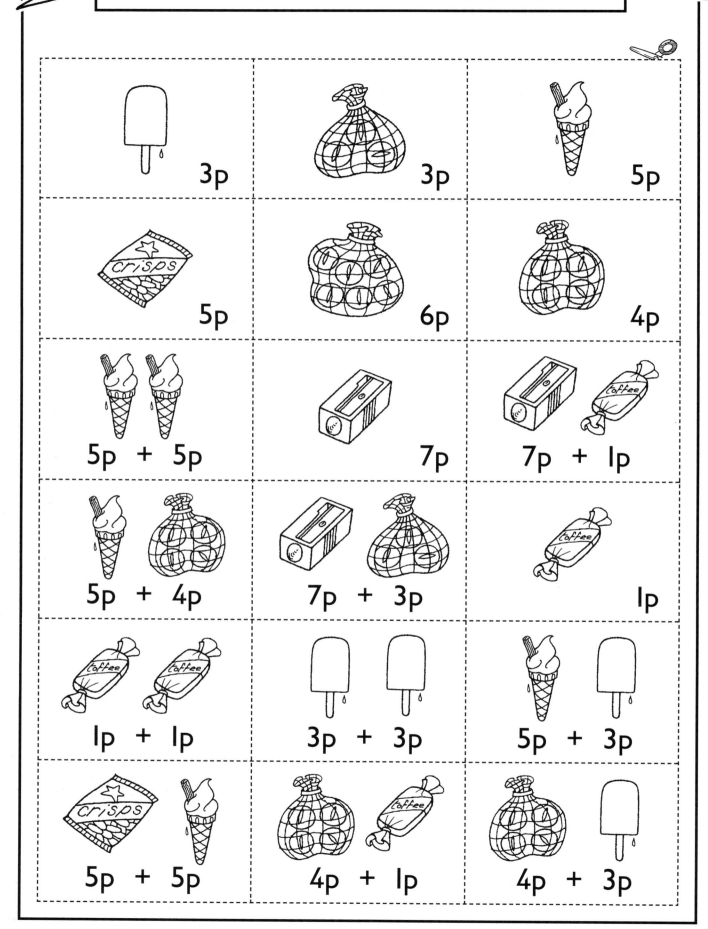

Teachers' note (Continued from page 63.) The children take turns to turn over a card from each set. If the amount in the purse is the same as the price of the shopping, they keep both cards. The winner is the one with the most pairs of cards when there are no cards left on the table. The children could also use the cards to play 'Snap'.

**Developing Numeracy
Solving Problems Year R**
© A & C Black